The
JICARILLA
APACHE

Shanahan, a Jicarilla Apache.

THE JICARILLA APACHE

A PORTRAIT

PHOTOGRAPHS BY
NANCY HUNTER WARREN

ESSAY BY
VERONICA E. VELARDE TILLER

UNIVERSITY OF NEW MEXICO PRESS
Albuquerque

Printed and bound in China through Four Colour Imports, Ltd.

YEAR   PRINTING

10 09 08 07 06   1 2 3 4 5

Library of Congress Cataloging-in-Publication Data

Warren, Nancy Hunter.
  The Jicarilla Apache : a portrait / illustrator, Nancy Hunter Warren ;
essay by Veronica E. Velarde Tiller.
      p. cm.
  Includes bibliographical references and index.
  ISBN-13: 978-0-8263-3775-7 (cloth : alk. paper)
  ISBN-10: 0-8263-3775-9 (cloth : alk. paper)
  ISBN-13: 978-0-8263-3776-4 (pbk. : alk. paper)
  ISBN-10: 0-8263-3776-7 (pbk. : alk. paper)
 1. Jicarilla Indians—New Mexico. 2. Jicarilla Indians—New Mexico—Pictoral works.
3. Jicarilla Indian Reservation (N.M.) 4. Jicarilla Indian Reservation (N.M.)—Pictoral works.
 I. Tiller, Veronica E. Velarde. II. Title.
  E99.J5W37 2006
  978.9'520049725—dc22
                            2006017260

Book design and composition by Damien Shay
Body type is Minion 12/18
Display is Bremen and Avant Garde

To

LUCIAN NIEMEYER

who shares my love
of photography
and helped make
this book possible.

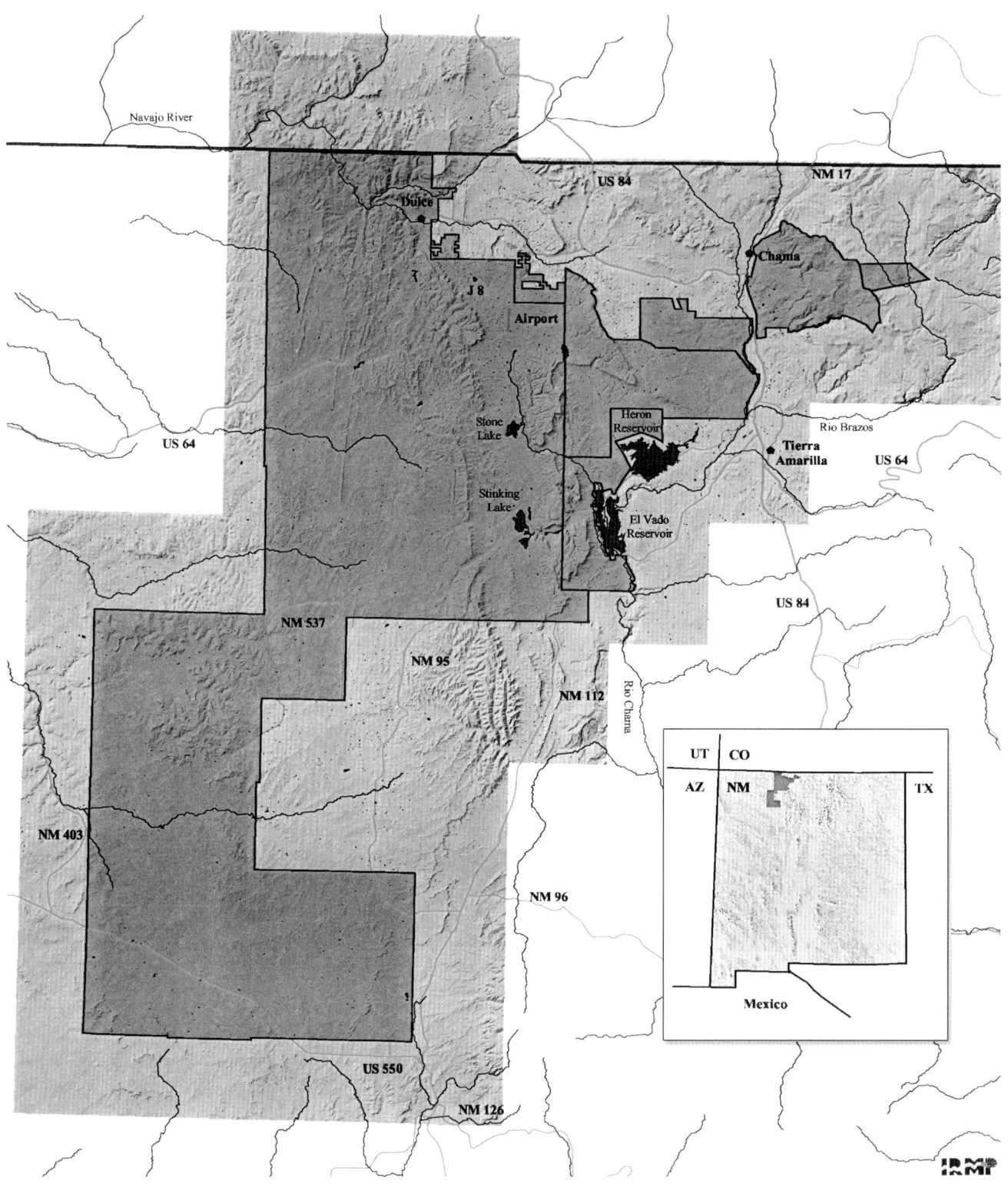

The Jicarilla Apache Nation Reservation in New Mexico. From the Jicarilla Apache Tribe's 1999 "Integrated Resource Management Plan." Courtesy of the Jicarilla Apache Tribe.

CONTENTS

LIST OF ILLUSTRATIONS

ANNUAL JICARILLA APACHE FOOT RACE

Moherita Veneno Largo at a picnic, 1981.

PREFACE

I met the Jicarillas in the fall of 1976. The occasion was the annual feast and foot race. I was invited by a friend of the Jicarillas. It was memorable for me—all so new and exciting. After the foot race, we went to the brush shelter shared by several Apache families. We were welcomed and they insisted on feeding us. I learned then that the best coffee in the world is made over a campfire. But best of all, they allowed me to photograph anything I wanted. Several of my favorite photographs came from this first visit.

For me, this was a unique and exhilarating occasion. I saw the foot race where the runners were decorated with paint and feathers, the beautiful teepees and brush shelters dotting the hills surrounding the racetrack, and smelled the wood smoke from many campfires.

At the time, it did not occur to me to make a book. I just wanted to capture on film what I saw. This visit was followed by many others. The photographs were all taken between 1976 and 1993. I came to know many other Jicarillas and to learn much of the lifestyles and customs. There were, of course, many things that I was not allowed to photograph. The Bear Dance and the Women's Coming Out were off limits. But I was allowed to observe and this was a real honor. The foot race was open to my camera during the 1970s and most of the '80s. But in later years if they asked me not to photograph I put my camera away. By now, the children are all grown up and there are many changes. But basically I think this portrait of the Jicarillas is still valid. The runners still compete in September, the dancers still

Julian home site near Dulce Rock, 1984.

gather from miles away, and Little Beaver still presides over his parade.

I've always been a Leica photographer with an occasional use of a Hasselblad. I have had three Leica cameras and I treasure their quiet ease of operation. The quality of their optics has given me sharpness in a well-balanced negative. Its ease of handling was important to me, photographing things such as the foot race,

powwow, or rodeo where fast movement was a problem. I am also a black and white photographer. For me, the abstracting qualities of black and white film are more compelling than color. In the darkroom there is a special joy and excitement in watching a print come to life in a tray of developer. For these reasons, my publications have almost always been done in black and white.

ACKNOWLEDGMENTS

I want to acknowledge and thank the following people for their part in making this book a reality:

Vance Packard, who built my first darkroom and who taught me the joy of photography.

My children, Bob, Janet, Scott, and Dan, for their love and support over the years.

Bobby Byrnes, who traveled countless miles with me to find and record the Jicarilla story. The Larry Julian and Bob Largo families for their kindness and patience in allowing me the privilege of photographing their lives.

Luther Wilson, director of UNM Press, for seeing the value in the book, and Damien Shay and Lisa Pacheco for their talented work in preparing this book for publication.

Special thanks to Lucian Niemeyer who spent many hours with me helping to make this book a reality.

Thanks also to Joan Niemeyer for her help and encouragement.

A chance meeting with Veronica Tiller many years ago led to this collaboration of photographs and text. Her sensitive words and clarity add understanding to the photographs. The story she tells will be an important addition to the historical record of the Jicarilla people. I am delighted to share this book with her.

Geraldine Julian at her ranch, 1982.

THE JICARILLA APACHE NATION TODAY

Veronica E. Velarde Tiller

Today, the Jicarilla Apache Reservation spans 836,207 acres of scenic terrain in north-central New Mexico. The reservation's northern boundary is also the Colorado state line. The north-south length of the reservation is about sixty miles long. It consists of two distinct areas that are physically and climatically different. The reservation's geography varies from high desert at the south boundary, at about six thousand five hundred feet in elevation, to mountainous areas of more than eleven thousand four hundred feet in elevation in the north. The average temperature on the reservation ranges from 38°F in winter to 83°F in summer. The average rainfall in the northern portion is about 17.4 inches per year, and snowfall averages 57 inches per year.

The northern portion of the Jicarilla Apache Reservation, consisting of approximately four hundred sixteen thousand acres, was created by the Executive Order of February 11, 1887. The southern portion consisting of approximately three hundred thousand acres was added by the Executive Orders of November 11, 1907 and January 28, 1908. Since the mid-1970s, the tribe has added about one hundred twenty thousand acres of land through the purchase of five ranches:

Steve Julian, 1977.

Theis, El Poso, Willow Creek, the Chama Land and Cattle Company, and the Gomez Ranch.

Most of the Jicarilla Apache Reservation lies north of U.S. Highway 550, which is the main route to the Four Corners area, and it is bisected north-south by State Highway 536. U.S. Highway 64 to Aztec and Farmington, U.S. Highway 64/84 to Chama, and U.S. Highway 84 to Pagosa Springs, Colorado, complete the major transportation corridors. There is access to the reservation via U.S. Highway 550 and State Highway 537. U.S. Highway 64/84, the corridor to the northeast through New Mexico and southern Colorado, carries most of the regional traffic but bypasses the reservation.

Tribal lands are abundant with natural resources, including forests, woodlands, lakes, streams, rivers, agricultural and range lands, and

Larry, a Jicarilla Apache—Jicarilla Apache Reservation, 1977.

oil and gas. A rich diversity of wildlife, including many species of furbearers, small game, and birds, makes the Jicarilla Reservation lands their home. Nearly fifty percent, or 404,837 acres, of the reservation is forested. Ponderosa pine represents the majority (more than ninety percent) of com-

mercial tree species. Harvesting occurs on the northern half of the reservation.

The Jicarilla Apache's tribal economy has long relied upon the use of the tribe's natural resources as its major source of revenue and employment. Harvesting oil, gas, and timber; ranching; tourism;

Aaron Manwell at his graduation from Dulce High School, 1977.

Forest ranger cabin at Stinking Lake, 1976.

Louise Pesata, a Jicarilla basket weaver, Dulce, 1979.

and hunting and fishing are the cornerstones of the tribal economy.

The tribe's wildlife and fisheries program is one of the largest and most respected fish and wildlife management initiatives on the continent. It manages a fourteen thousand five hundred-acre game park and has implemented a number of projects that preserve the wildlife population and, at the same time, create a significant source of rev-enue for the tribe. The fish stock in tribal waters include rainbow, brook, brown, and cutthroat trout; bluehead sucker, flannelmouth sucker, speckled dace, and mottled sculpin. Reservation lakes are restocked annually with about one hundred thousand fish, and the larger lakes are managed as "put, grow, and take" sites. Annual gill netting surveys are conducted at the lakes, and populations are monitored closely.

A Navajo woman shearing sheep at the Julian Ranch, 1982.

The reservation offers the outdoor enthusiast and tourist some of the most spectacular vacation, sightseeing, sports, hunting, and fishing opportunities in the southwestern United States. For the sportsman, hunting on the reservation is considered some of the best in the United States, drawing hunters and sightseers worldwide. Five major big game (elk and deer) migration corridors cross the reservation. Game includes elk, black bear, mountain lion, turkey, and Canadian geese. In addition, seven of the tribe's fifteen mountain lakes are stocked with rainbow, brown, and cutthroat trout. Fishing is permitted at Dulce, Enbom, Hayden, Horse, La Jara, Mundo, and Stone Lakes, and the Navajo River. The tribe welcomes all visitors, but it requires that they abide by guidelines and restrictions intended to protect and preserve natural resources.

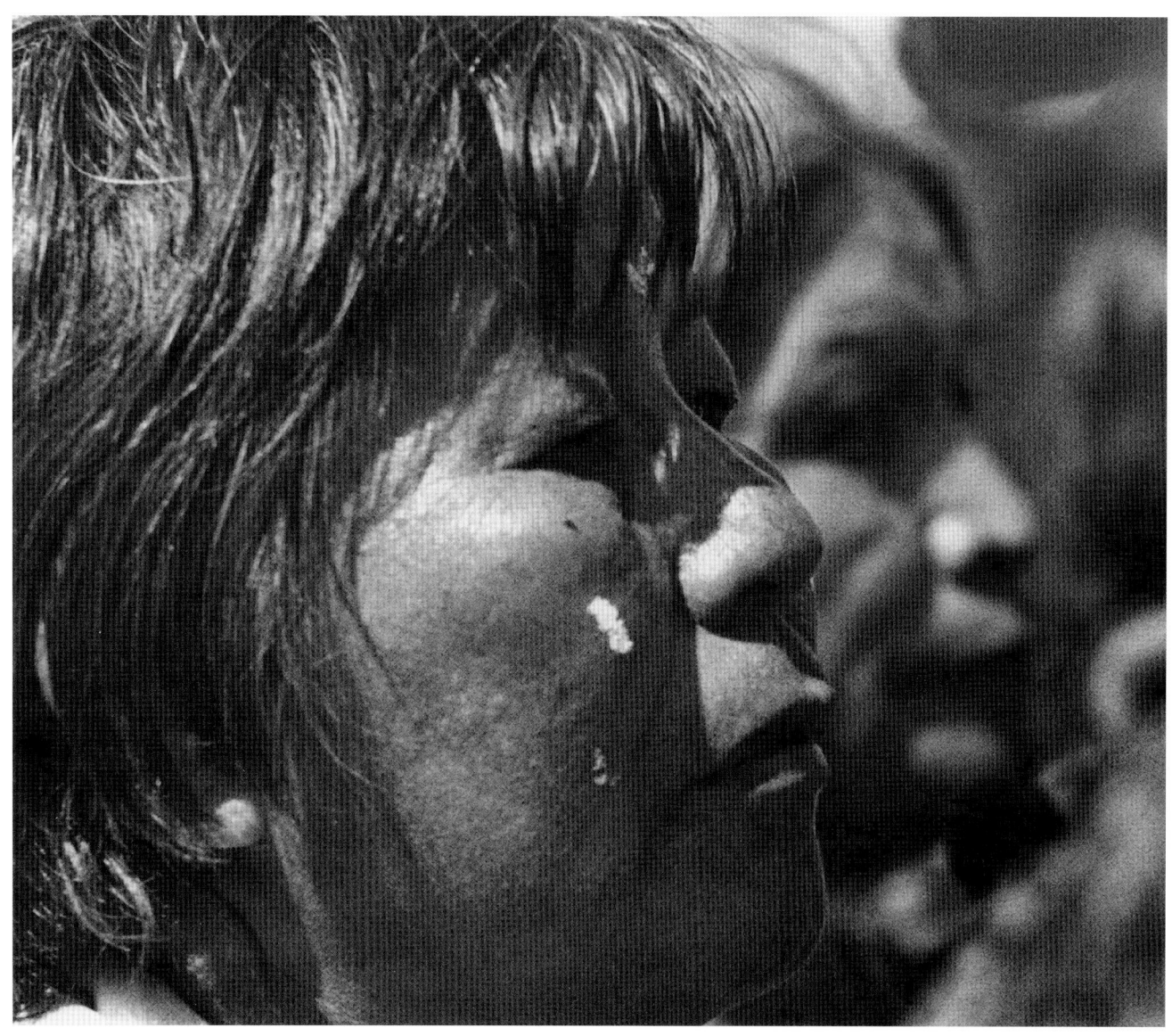

Helen Lovato and Rebecca Monarco Martinez at Go-Jii-Yah, 1977.

Vondeevee Julian, 1981.

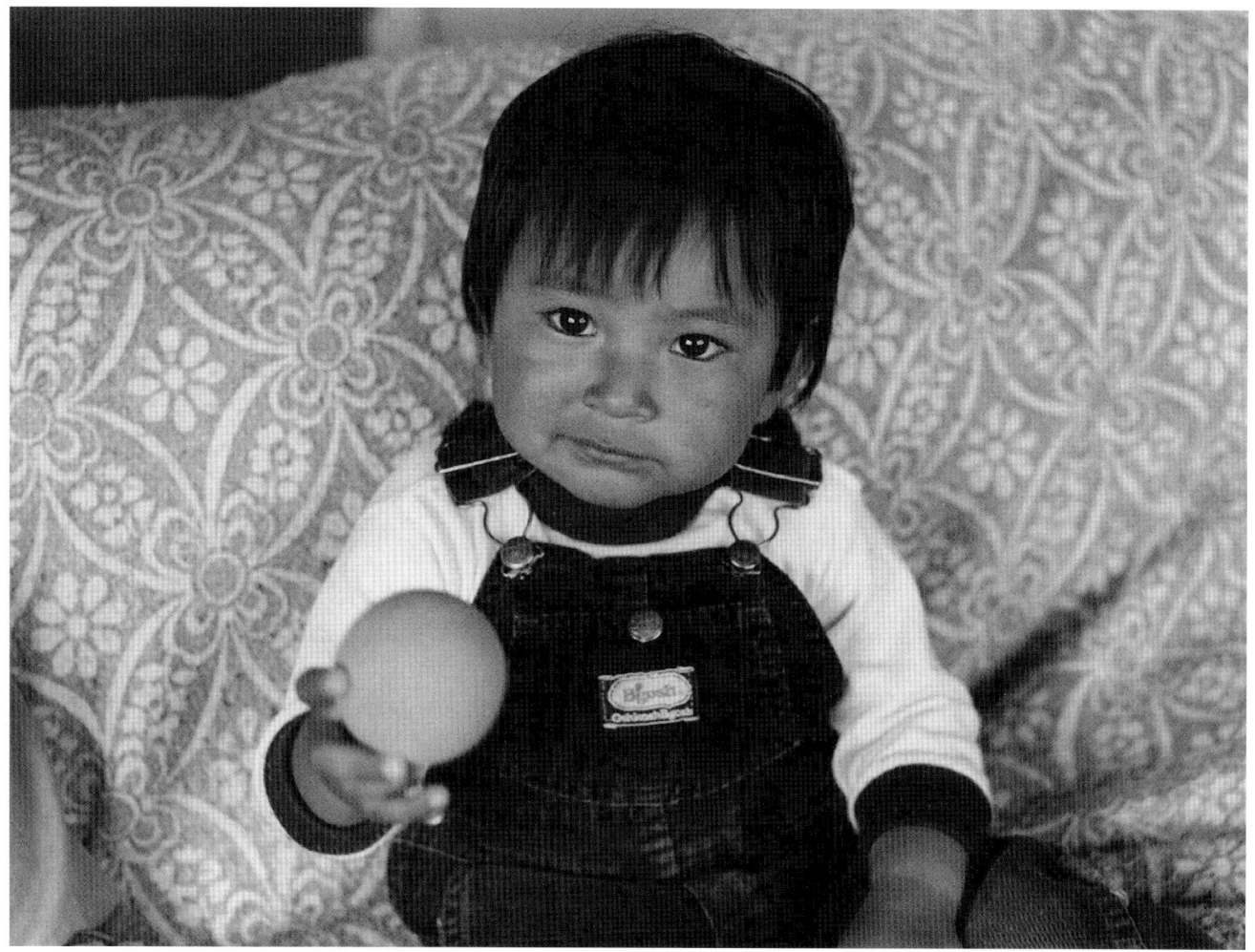

Tyrell Largo, 1981.

The Jicarilla Apache Reservation is geographically situated in the resource-rich San Juan Basin, which contains the second-largest gas field in the continental United States and is the largest producer of oil of any basin in the Rocky Mountains. The basin contains large amounts of oil, gas, coal, uranium, and geothermal reserves. Coal underlies nearly all of the reservation, and oil and gas pools underlie the southern portion of the reservation. The Jicarilla Apache Tribe was the first United States tribe to acquire and operate its own oil and gas production company. The tribe bought out the interests of a private sector partner in 1977, becoming the sole owner of the company. The Jicarilla Apache Tribe is the single largest mineral owner in the San Juan Basin, excluding the U.S.

The Julian Home in Dulce, 1981.

government. During more than thirty-five years of gas and oil activity on the reservation, more than two thousand seven hundred wells have been drilled. The tribe's most important source of revenue stems from its mineral reserves.

The reservation's ample natural resources have proven to be the tribe's greatest economic asset. The tribe operates a number of enterprises that contribute to the tribal economy. Its ventures in the agriculture, forestry, gaming, mining, retail, and tourism industries provide a great source of income for the tribe and help support both the tribal and local economies. Government jobs account for about fifty percent of the employment for tribal members. The livestock industry has been a primary use of reservation land since

Everett Quintana, Dulce, 1977.

1890. Ranching serves as the main agricultural enterprise on the Jicarilla Apache Reservation and features many family-operated, cow-calf operations. Sheep raising dominated this industry until 1960 when cattle raising increased.

HISTORY AND CULTURE

Scholars believe that Apache people migrated from arctic regions of western Canada to the desert southwest of the United States between the late thirteenth and sixteenth centuries. The Jicarilla Apache people's traditional lands spanned more than 50 million acres and were bounded by four sacred rivers. Traditional territories included portions of Texas, Colorado, and New Mexico. The Apache people, including those on the Jicarilla Apache Reservation, are linguistically related to the greater Na-Dene language family.

Jicarilla band (Apache Ramblers) playing in Dulce, 1977.

The Apaches vehemently resisted the encroachment upon their traditional lands by Spanish, Mexican, and American settlers and military forces. But by the mid-1880s, Apaches were consolidated on various southwestern Indian reservations. The Jicarillas were sent to the Mescalero Apache Reservation in southeastern New Mexico.

Jicarilla tribal leadership, stepping outside the bounds of traditional channels, sought to win the support of New Mexico Territorial Governor Ross in 1886 in an attempt to regain their northern reservation. Ross's influential coalition convinced the president to sign the Executive Order of February 8, 1887, which created the permanent site of the Jicarilla Apache Reservation.

A Jicarilla Apache shepherd in Dulce.

Martha Jean Gonzales.

Vondeevee Julian flying a kite.

GOVERNMENT

The Jicarilla Apache adopted their original constitution and bylaws on August 4, 1937 under the terms of the Indian Reorganization Act of 1934. This constitution was revised in 1968. In 2000 the Jicarilla Apache Tribe officially changed its name to the Jicarilla Apache Nation. The Jicarilla Apache tribal government consists of three branches: the legislative, executive, and judicial. The legislative branch is composed of a legislative council consisting of eight members who serve staggered terms of four years. The executive branch consists of a president and vice president,

Martha Jean Gonzales, 1978.

Geraldine Julian, beadworker.

who are also elected every four years by tribal members eighteen years of age and older. The president appoints the secretary and treasurer. The judiciary branch consists of a tribal court with up to two judges appointed by the president and an appellate court consisting of three members of the legislative council also appointed by the president.

The popular image of the Indian people throughout the United States is that their lives are generally miserable due to poor social and economic conditions. While conditions have not always been the best, Indian people have always had reasons to be thankful, to celebrate, and have fun. The Jicarilla Apache are no different; their

Chickens at Julian Ranch.

Kirk Amarillo, Robert Largo, and William Vicenti on float in Parade, 1978.

lives consist of celebrations and festivities. Some celebrations are culturally based in that they have been part of Jicarilla Apache culture before Columbus came to America, while others like the Little Beaver Celebration are an adaptation of western American tradition.

THE LITTLE BEAVER PARADE

One of the highlights of the Little Beaver Celebration is the parade. Every year the Little Beaver Committee develops a theme. Themes usually reflect what is happening in the larger society or something important to the tribe. A recurring theme is the promotion of education. One year the theme had to do with Saddam Hussein during the U.S. Gulf War. A grand marshal is selected to head the parade and throughout its history it has been a popular politician, like current New Mexico Governor Bill Richardson (then U.S. Representative of northern New Mexico), or one of the tribe's attorneys from Albuquerque, but most likely an important member from within the tribe.

Carnival at Little Beaver Celebration, 1977.

In June 2004, Troy Vicenti, the original "Little Beaver," by tribal proclamation was recognized as the co-grand marshal for each year of the celebration. Troy Vicenti, at the age of ten, became the first Little Beaver to ride with Fred Harman. Later his son, Jason Vicenti, also served as Little Beaver. Many young boys have served as the Little Beaver over the years. A competition is held to determine which young boy, from ages eight to twelve, will serve as Little Beaver. The qualifications are the ability to ride a horse bareback and a willingness to serve as the tribe's representative to area events, such as rodeos and parades.

Other rodeo royalty are selected along with Little Beaver, mainly the rodeo queen and her attendants. By the 1970s, with the national Indian rights movement and resurgence of Indian identity as a backdrop, the Little Beaver Celebration

Little Beaver Parade in Dulce, 1991.

added another category of royalties, Miss Jicarilla and Jr. Miss Jicarilla and their courts. Lillian Caramillo was crowned as the first Miss Jicarilla in 1974. Since her reign, at least thirty Jicarilla young ladies have served in this capacity.

THE LITTLE BEAVER ROUNDUP

A testimonial to the love of rodeo is the annual Little Beaver Roundup that takes place usually the third weekend in July in Dulce. Known as the Little Beaver Celebration today, this annual event offers a variety of activities such as the rodeo, pony express race, powwow, parade, softball tournament, carnival, and art show. It is a public event open to everyone. It begins with a parade on Saturday morning. This is a typical, rural, western American tradition that was adopted lock, stock, and barrel by the Indian people. Little Beaver began in 1958 when Fred Harman of

Roland Smith, Jr. as Little Beaver in annual Parade—Dulce, 1993.

Pagosa Springs, Colorado, encouraged the tribal council to expand its rodeo to include a parade and other events. Fred Harman was portraying the western comic character, Red Ryder, whose "Indian sidekick" was Little Beaver. In his honor, the town of Pagosa celebrates the Red Ryder Roundup during the Fourth of July. After 1958 the Little Beaver Roundup, as it was first known, was expanded to include a host of other events.

THE LITTLE BEAVER CELEBRATION POWWOW

While tribal dances have always been a historical part of the Jicarilla social scene, a powwow that was widely advertised inviting all Indian tribes to the Little Beaver Celebration did not occur until the mid-1970s. The Jicarilla powwow staged during the Little Beaver Celebration was

Sad Aim Hussein float in the Little Beaver Parade, 1991.

a part of the national phenomenon whereby Indian tribes and peoples began to look more to their own culture and heritage as the reason for tribal celebrations rather than just the celebration tied to the western American-oriented activities, like rodeos. Nationwide throughout Indian country, powwows became very popular events.

Many Indian people traveled throughout the United States competing in the dancing events and Dulce was only one stop along the yearly powwow circuit. In turn many Jicarilla families went to other tribal festivals and powwows to enjoy the events and to compete in the powwows. One popular event in northern New Mexico is the

Sherman Julian, 1979.

Julians' spaceship float in the Little Beaver Parade—Dulce, 1978.

Little Beaver Parade in Dulce, 1993.

Wyns and Tyrell Largo at Stone Lake, 1982.

Last float in the Little Beaver Parade—Dulce, 1978.

Taos Powwow, which draws visitors from throughout the world and nation. Historically, Jicarilla people have always had a close relationship with the Pueblo of Taos. Friendships between the two tribes began many generations ago and continue to this day. The Jicarillas share the foot race with the Taos and Picuris Pueblos of north-ern New Mexico. On August 9 and September 30 each year, these two Pueblos also have their own foot races. The race in Taos is part of the San Geronimo Feast Day. In the old days, after Go-Jii-Yah was over, the Jicarilla people set out for Taos, often by horse and wagon, to attend San Geronimo Day.

Go-Jii-Yah Rodeo at Stone Lake, 1977.

THE POWWOW

In the afternoon of the September 15 celebration, after the foot races and lunch, two other events take place: the dances or powwow at the center of the campgrounds, where concession stands are set up. In the earlier days, this time was for social dancing, when everyone got dressed in their traditional regalia and had a good time. The round dance was the popular social dance during Go-Jii-Yah during that period. It took place in the evenings and continued until the early morning hours. On the early evening of the fourteenth both clans have dances on the racetrack.

It was not until about the 1970s when the dancing became a powwow, in the modern sense, and prize money was awarded to the best dancers in various categories. The powwow is usually managed by a tribal committee, and is often advertised as an independent event throughout nearby Indian Country. This powwow has attracted many Indian visitors from as far away as South Dakota, but mainly from neighboring tribes. It still draws a large crowd and audience.

Spectators at Little Beaver Roundup Rodeo, 1977.

Bullrider and clown at Little Beaver Rodeo.

THE RODEO

While the powwow is going on, at the nearby rodeo grounds Indian cowboys and cowgirls and non-Indian cowboys and cowgirls compete in rodeo events, mainly calf roping, team roping, bareback and saddle bronc riding, and barrel racing. This rural, western ranching tradition is strong on Indian reservations throughout America. For the Jicarillas, the love of horses and the competitive atmosphere is the attraction. The horse is a venerable animal in Jicarilla life, both

spiritually and economically. The rodeo was added to the September 15 celebration in the late 1940s when roping, riding, and horse racing were the main events. The original rodeo grounds were located a few hundred yards west of the road that leads from Stone to Stinking Lake, directly across from Stone Lake. It was moved to its current location (near Stone Lake, nineteen miles south of Dulce) during the 1970s.

The sport of rodeo is tied to the history of the Jicarilla reservation's settlement and economic development. In 1887 when the Jicarilla Apache

Kenneth Dedios, Jr. roping at Go-Jii-Yah Rodeo, 1990.

were settled on the northern portion of the Jicarilla Reservation, the federal government had intended for all Jicarillas to become farmers according to a generic formula outlined in the Dawes Act of 1887. This federal legislation mandated that all Indian tribesmen become assimilated into mainstream American society. The means for reaching that goal was for Indians to become farmers on land allotments of 160–640 acres. The problem with this formula for the Jicarillas was that the climate, terrain, and availability of water resources on the northern New Mexico reservation were not conducive to farming. The federal experiment failed miserably but redemption appeared on the horizon by the 1920s when sheep were issued to all heads of families. Like ducks taking to water, the Jicarillas became excellent livestock owners and by the 1940s, numerous sheep and cattle operations dotted the reservation. There were large numbers

Young dancer at the powwow in Dulce, 1987.

Calf roper practicing on bale of hay with horns, 1976.

of Jicarilla families who owned large livestock businesses. During World War II, the Jicarilla live-stock owners were possibly on par with the rest of the state of New Mexico in terms of personal income from ranching and livestock raising because of the demand for food products. The decline of this industry began with the severe droughts of the 1950s.

With an increase in family ranch incomes during the 1940s, many families embraced the sport of rodeo and a new tradition grew up among the ranching people. Ranching families could now afford to buy horses for rodeo competition and travel to rodeos throughout New Mexico and Colorado. This recreational sport was a natural development; it reinforced the Jicarilla love of the outdoors, working with and caring for animals, and they had the lifestyle to support it.

In the 1970s and 1980s the rodeo was especially popular. While the reservation populace was centered in Dulce by the 1970s, there were a handful of families that still ranched and it was these families that led the rodeo craze. Coming from the southern portion of the reservation was cattle

Young dancer at the powwow in Dulce, 1991.

Wilbur Montoya and team roping partner at Go-Jii-Yah Rodeo.

rancher, Kenneth Dedios, and his sons, Kenneth Jr. and Willard whose recreational lives centered on team roping. The young Kenneth pictured in this book (page 33) became a very successful competitor at national team roping events. Kenneth's two other brothers, Richard and Nathaniel Dedios, were also active in the sport. For Lindberg and Bob Velarde, both ranchers (and brothers) from the Lindrith area on the southern portion of the reservation, the sport of rodeo was a long-standing family tradition. Their father, Albert Velarde, Sr., led a group of Jicarilla ranch hands, including his close

friend, Stephen Vicenti, to initiate rodeo as part of Go-Jii-Yah back in the 1940s. During the 1970s and '80s a weekend didn't go by without Lindberg, his wife, Maxine, and their sons, Albert III and Wrighty, being present at some rodeo. Maxine became one of the first women team ropers, roping with her husband and sons. Bob Velarde, an avid calf and team roper, was joined by his wife, Bette, and daughter, BobbiNell.

The ranching family of the Elotes—consisting of Harrison and his sons, Meryl and Erwin—from the La Jara Canyon/Pound's Mill area of the

Powwow at Taos Pueblo, 1989.

Powwow—Jicarilla dancer in Dulce, 1988.

Steve Julian practicing his roping—Dulce, 1977.

reservation, were also team ropers. Many rodeo participants by the 1970s and '80s were not ranchers or livestock owners, but came from a long line of ranching families like the Serafin brothers, Everett and Lucien. Their father, Theodore Serafin, was the owner of one of the largest sheep ranches at Campanero Canyon up to the mid-1960s. The Jicarilla Tribal government was a great supporter of tourism and recreation. Rodeo was one activity that was sponsored by the tribe, in part because two team ropers, Harrison Elote and Edwin Sandoval, were members of the

council in the 1970s and early 1980s. In addition to the roping, there are a host of Jicarilla cowboys who specialize in the riding event, and Jicarilla cowgirls who barrel race and team rope.

Go-Jii-Yah is the final Jicarilla event that marks the beginning of the fall and winter seasons, when everyone returns to their homes and jobs. Up through the early 1950s livestock owners began moving their herds to the southern portion of the reservation where the climate is warmer and livestock can better survive the winters. Today, the majority of Jicarilla tribal members return to the

Opening the chute. Little Beaver Rodeo—Dulce, 1990.

comforts of their modern homes and to their jobs, while visitors and off-reservation tribal residents also return to their places of residence.

THE COMMUNITY OF DULCE

As the livestock industry declined during the early 1960s, the wage earning opportunities offered by the tribe improved and with it the town of Dulce grew. The tribe's income from oil and gas increased as well as federal aid for housing, social services, tribal governmental operations, and health serv-

ices. The town of Dulce was where the federal government set up the first Jicarilla Apache Indian Agency as its headquarters. The reason Dulce became the agency's headquarters was that the Denver Rio Grande Railroad line came through the northernmost part of the reservation. In the 1880s, the Jicarilla Apache Agency received its supplies, including food rations that were disbursed to all Jicarilla families. The railroad was the most convenient means of transporting goods to this isolated Indian agency. As the livestock industry grew, the railroads were used to ship sheep, lambs,

Dancer at Taos Pueblo Powwow, 1993.

Taos Pueblo Powwow, 1987.

and cattle to market. This main railroad line had spurs from Dulce southward along Embom, Stone, and Stinking Lakes. These spurs lead to the interior of the reservation where the tribe's major timber resources were once located. One would never know that there had been an abundance of timber from Dulce to Stone Lake because by the 1920s, the land was completely denuded by the horrendous practice of clear-cutting forestlands that

the government allowed on Indian lands. The upside of this environmental disaster was that the timber provided the government with revenue for the purchase of livestock for the Jicarilla people.

The Navajo River, just over the hill north of Dulce and below Archuleta Peak, is the source of water for the town. It is because of the proximity to this valuable water resource that the town of Dulce still exists and on which its historic

Calf roper at Go-Jii-Yah Rodeo.

growth has been predicated. Because of the rail-road and its closeness to the Navajo River, the town of Dulce was established in the 1890s. Dulce has become a hub of commerce, the tribe's headquarters, and where three of every four Jicarilla tribal members live today.

By the 1960s, there was a trend of families moving into Dulce to take advantage of the employment opportunities afforded by tribal government. Many Dulce families continued to have small live-stock operations throughout the reservation. Two such families were the Largos and Julians who live in Dulce near the Little Beaver Rodeo Grounds. Larry Julian and his wife, Geraldine, own the Julian JS Ranch located on the Navajo River. Both Larry and his wife have held many tribal jobs through-out their lives but have continued to hold on to their ranch. Today they still raise cattle and their ranch has been a focal point for family gatherings; a place for the children of the extended family to

Saddle bronc rider at Little Beaver Rodeo.

visit, to have fun, and assist with ranching chores. The Largos and Julians are representative of Jicarilla tribal members who live in Dulce. They work for the tribe, live near Dulce, but continue to ranch on the nearby Navajo River and actively participate in Go-Jii-Yah and the Little Beaver Celebration. Robert Largo even had a band that rode in the Little Beaver Parade for many years.

The first decade of the twenty-first century finds the town of Dulce still growing. All businesses located within the town of Dulce are tribally owned. Several new businesses opened in 2004. The newly built and modern Jicarilla Apache Supermarket has a deli-café, a bakery, a Wells Fargo Bank branch, and a community meeting room. A new hardware store affiliated with TruValue also opened in 2004. Apache House of Liquors, a Conoco station with a convenience store, the Jicarilla station, and the Best Western Jicarilla Inn are long-standing businesses. The inn

Women dancers at the powwow in Dulce, 1987.

Cowboy spectators at Go-Jii-Yah Rodeo, 1977.

offers excellent accommodations, includes a restaurant and lounge, and a gift shop with original art.

The Jicarilla Apache Arts and Crafts Museum is a tribal department that promotes the preservation of traditional arts and crafts by employing and training Apache artisans and through its sales. It exhibits historical baskets, photographs, paintings, and clothing. Many Jicarilla women are employees at the Jicarilla Museum, serving as basketmakers and beaders. They are more like artists-in-residence due

to their skills and artistic abilities. One woman who is a well-known Jicarilla basketmaker is Louise Pesata (page 6), a life-long resident of the reservation. Currently her son, Levi Pesata, is serving as the president of the Jicarilla Apache Nation.

Dulce has a multipurpose community center that houses tribal offices, a bowling alley, a swimming pool, and a gymnasium. There is a senior citizen center with dining facilities, meeting space, and an office. A cultural center with a gift shop is

Raynard, Derrick Valdez, and Terrance Julian at Julian Ranch
on Navajo River, 1980.

located in an office in the historic district. Recreational facilities include a lighted rodeo arena with nearby camping facilities, a lighted baseball field, and a park. A new, fully equipped fitness center was opened in 2000. Many recreational facilities are shared with the local public school, such as the football stadium with a padded track for field sports and recreational walking. The U.S. Postal Service built a new post office in 2002. There is also a fire department and a library.

Jicarilla youth in grades K–12 attend the local public elementary, middle, and high schools in the Dulce School District. The tribe has an education department that sponsors programs such as higher education, adult education, cultural and language preservation, a library, and federal programs. The tribe began the Chester E. Faris Scholarship program for higher education in 1952 with its first proceeds from the discovery of oil and gas. In 2002, in honor of a venerated elder,

Cattle branding on the Julian Ranch on Navajo River, 1980.

the program changed its name to the Norman TeCube Sr. Scholarship Fund.

The department also provides a cultural preservation program. The program's goal is to promote language retention, develop curriculum, and teach cultural crafts and stories. Language, art, and culture classes are offered in the Dulce school system, St. Francis School, and the tribal education programs. A language immersion program is held in the Dulce Day Care Center. The program's other projects include adult Jicarilla language classes and a culture camp.

The photographs in this book provide only a small window into the lives of the Jicarilla Apache in the 1970s and 1980s and portray another important aspect of Jicarilla life: celebrations both old and new. They also portray the lives of everyday Jicarilla people who make up the tribe. Nancy Warren is to be commended for her excellent photographs that will become even more

(L to R) Kenneth Dedios, Lindberg, Bette, Bob, and Wrighty Velarde
at Go-Jii-Yah Rodeo, 1977.

important as time goes on because they preserve Jicarilla history and her efforts will encourage others to document history through photographs and to understand that history is really about people.

THE SEPTEMBER 14–15 *GO-JII-YAH* FEAST

Echoing through the canyons and mountains of northern New Mexico are the voices of modern Apache people singing ancient songs and carrying out ancient obligatory rituals in modern ways.

Every year on September 14 and 15, the people who call themselves Jicarilla Apache come together to celebrate the symbolic, ceremonial foot race between the two clans: the *Olleros* and *Llaneros*, also referred to as the White and Red Clans, respectively. They camp out at Stone Lake, about twenty miles from the town of Dulce, the headquarters of the Jicarilla Apache Nation. Dulce is only a fifteen-minute drive from Stone Lake and yet the lure of being at Stone Lake is so strong that almost all families make the effort to camp out. The days September 14 and 15 are official tribal

Dancer at the powwow in Dulce, 1979.

holidays, like Christmas, Memorial Day, and the Fourth of July are for all Americans.

This race was mandated by the First People. It was said that every year without fail this ceremony had to take place. Since the Jicarilla people settled on the Jicarilla Apache Reservation in 1887, this ceremony has taken place. And long before

that time. The purpose of the ceremonial event has remained the same but the way it is celebrated has changed over time. It has been referred to by various names: Go-Jii-Yah in Apache, a fiesta by visitors, September Fifteenth by locals, and a ceremonial relay race by anthropologists. No matter what it is called, it is a celebration of the past,

Powwow at Dulce, 1981.

the present, and the future. Every Jicarilla Apache, no matter his or her religious persuasion, participates in some aspect of this annual celebration. It is the one single event that brings the people together every year and it is the event that every Jicarilla Apache identifies with in some way.

The beauty of this event is that it is many things to different people. And because it means so many different things to all Jicarillas, it has sur-

vived as the premier tribal celebration and it continues to take place every year. For those Jicarilla people who still practice their native religion, it is primarily a religious event, a spiritual time of reconnection with the Creator and the forces of nature. It is a special day of thanksgiving for all the gifts of life and for hopes and dreams that came true. It is a time when Jicarillas give thanks for the bounty of the earth, the moon and stars

Jicarilla Apache drummers at the powwow in Dulce, 1991.

in the sky, the clouds that bring the rain and snow, the wind that blows, the plants that grow, the animals that share the earth with us, and for the sun, without which there is no life.

It is not only a celebration for the renewal of faith, but a time to reconnect with family, and a time to celebrate our very existence as a tribe. This celebration is indeed a true Jicarilla tradition. Unlike the rest of American society, where family reunions take place about every ten years, Go-Jii-Yah is the tribe's annual family reunion and

camp-out. It is not uncommon to see Jicarilla families start setting up their campsites as early as Labor Day weekend. In the earlier days, when livestock raising was the primary occupation of Jicarilla people, they brought their sheep and goat herds to the Stone Lake area and camped out for as long as a week. Friends and visitors from Navajo and Pueblo country came from miles away on wagons, horseback, and later on, in trucks and cars. They camped with or near their Apache host families. It was a time to trade goods; Jicarilla beef

Jicarilla Apache drummer at the powwow in Dulce.

Little Beaver Parade in Dulce.

and mutton products for fruit and vegetables or silver jewelry and blankets. It was a grand time to celebrate just before everyone went their separate ways for the winter months.

By the mid-1970s, it seemed only our die-hard Indian friends from other tribes attended this Jicarilla celebration. For one thing, the New Mexico State Fair is in full swing by September 14th and that has become more of an attraction for the Indians of New Mexico. By the 1970s, many Jicarilla students began attending colleges and universities and many sought employment outside the reservation. Depending on where these off-reservation members lived, they made the annual trek or pilgrimage back home to the reservation for this event. For them this was a homecoming. In 1976, I for one had just moved to Salt Lake City, Utah, to begin my college teaching career. My daughter Emily and I made the trip to Stone Lake to join our family. For more than

Young dancer at Little Beaver Powwow in Dulce, 1989.

Moherita Largo and Geraldine Julian on picnic.

fifty years I have attended this ceremony, driving from Salt Lake City and Albuquerque, and flying in from Washington, D.C. In 1976 my siblings were living in Albuquerque, Tucson, Denver, and San Francisco, and we all made it to Stone Lake.

My cousin, Ester Hassall, who married a career Navy man, moved and lived all over the world but has managed to make it to Go-Jii-Yah along with her husband, David, and their children on a regular basis.

Llaneros dancing prior to start of race at Stone Lake, 1980.

Jicarilla Apache Tribal Feast Grounds at Stone Lake, 1980.

THE FOOT RACE

Veronica E. Velarde Tiller

The race takes place on September 15 around 10 a.m. on a one-third-mile, east-west racetrack. The two clan runners line up and race until the losing side acknowledges defeat. It is a time of initiation for young boys who run in the race. It is a time for old men to find out whether they can still run the course. It is a challenge; it is competition, but most of all it is symbolic of the original race between the Sun and Moon. The event focuses on adolescent boys. This is their event. Young adolescent girls, by contrast, are honored during their puberty feasts that take place throughout the summer months on the reservation. These days, most

Llanero runners line up—Go-Jii-Yah, Stone Lake, 1980.

anyone can run, including friends and visitors especially on the White side. A head runner is selected on the evening of the fourteenth where each clan holds trials. It is truly an honor to be selected as the head runner. This runner has the responsibility to run as many times during the race as necessary to bring victory for his clansmen. Providing the leadership and guidance for the conduct of the race are Jicarilla men from both clans. These experienced spiritual leaders, themselves, have been runners as young boys. Over time they have served as apprentices to the older men and have learned the ways and means for assisting in managing the race.

The Ollero Clan, traditionally, was made up of families from livestock ranching families.

Ollero and Llanero Runners at the starting line—Go-Jii-Yah, 1976.

They lived in areas like La Jara, Horse Lake, Stinking Lake, Hillcrest, Campanero Canyon, Dulce Lake, and Stone Lake areas. The Llanero members were primarily from the town of Dulce, its surrounding areas, and Sawmill Canyon. Historically the Olleros were the mountain-valley Apaches, whose traditional homelands were the mountain-valley areas of northeastern New Mexico, and they had a strong tradition as horticulturists. The Llaneros were the plains Apaches. Llanero means "plainsman" in the Spanish language. In the late nineteenth century, just prior to the removal of the Jicarilla Apache to the 1887 Executive Order Reservation, the Olleros lived around Abiquiu and the Llaneros lived near Cimarron, both in northeastern New Mexico. The Llaneros have always outnumbered the Olleros by a

Tweety Muniz, Llanero runner at Go-Jii-Yah—Stone Lake, 1980.

Clyde Gomez, Llanero runner at Go-Jii-Yah—Stone Lake, 1988.

Jicarilla Apache runner at Go-Jii-Yah—Stone Lake, 1977.

three-to-one ratio. Upon location on the reservation, the Llaneros chose areas close to the Jicarilla agency site, while Olleros tended to live throughout the rest of the reservation.

When the winning side is declared the race is over. The losing side beats the drum and the racers join their respective clans and the rivalry ends. The two clans dance down the track toward their two respective kivas at each end of the racetrack. As the two rivals come together at about the center of the racetrack, food and candy are tossed into the air for everyone to catch. The purpose of this

Llanero runners with Travis Chavez at Go-Jii-Yah—Stone Lake, 1991.

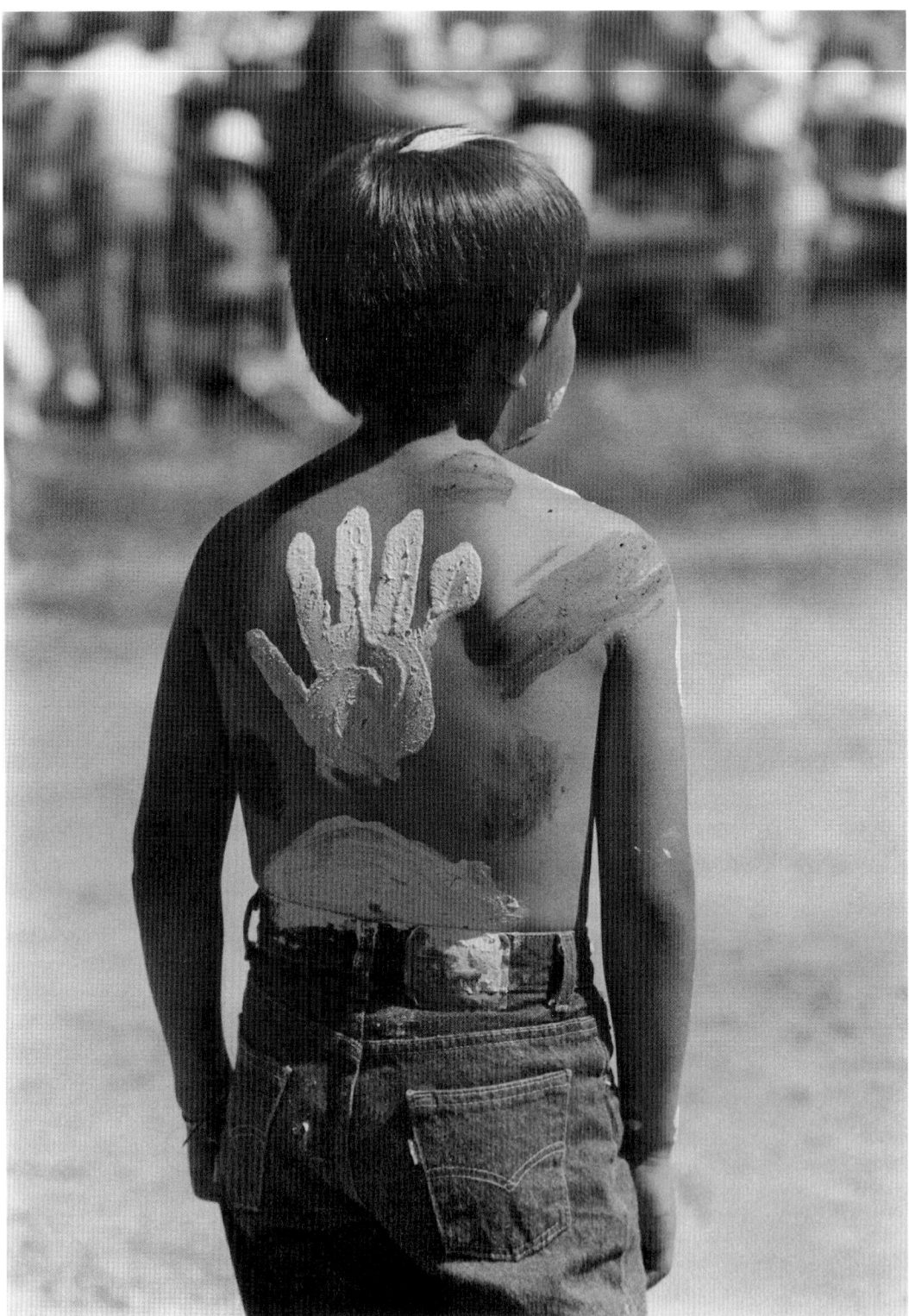

Young Apache runner at Go-Jii-Yah—Stone Lake, 1990.

Llanero runner with Travis Chavez at Go-Jii-Yah—Stone Lake, 1983.

Jicarilla Apache runner at end of the race—Go-Jii-Yah, 1990.

Ollero runner at Go-Jii-Yah.

is a symbolic gesture of celebrating the bounty of the earth. When Jicarilla people were ranchers and farmers, they threw food grown in home gardens, like ears of corn, melons, and apples, but today it is primarily store-bought candy and fruit. The two sides continue down to their kivas where songs and prayers are given.

One memorable Ollero person at the center of the racetrack, gaily dancing next to the Ollero flag bearer with her familiar smile and huge load of mixed fruit and vegetables on her back, was Petklo Romero Garcia (pages 70, 74, 77), the first lady of Go-Jii-Yah for the decades of the '50s, '60s, and into the '70s. The women of the Ollero Clan participate in the dancing prior to and after the race, while the Llanero women do not. Petklo, as she was popularly known, was from La Jara Canyon where she and

Petklo Garcia, Ollero dancer, Osborn Velarde, Ollero flag bearer, 1978.

Olleros and Llaneros meet at end of race at mid-track celebrating
by tossing foodstuff, 1978.

The red and white flags are the pennants of the two clans—Stone Lake, 1978.

Philbert Vigil, Jr., Ollero runner at Go-Jii-Yah—Stone Lake, 1990.

her husband ran a herd of sheep and goats until his death in the late 1950s.

Petklo was the quintessential Jicarilla woman, with strong religious beliefs and caretaker of her extended family and tribe. In many ways her life exemplified what a Jicarilla woman is supposed to be: kind and generous, caring and dignified, responsible, smart, and the standard bearer of the best of Jicarilla traditional values and beliefs. For several decades,

Petklo staged a puberty feast for all of her female grandchildren and provided the entire tribe with a social gathering every summer near her home. This four-day event is a costly event but Petklo could always rely on her tribesmen to help her out with sheep and cattle for meat, potatoes, flour, coffee, the manpower for the hauling of water, the supply of wood for the cook fires, etc. Of course, every medicine man was honored to perform the ceremony with no

Ollero women: Petklo Garcia and Belle Wells at Go-Jii-Yah—Stone Lake, 1990.

Ollero women: (L to R) Belle Wells, Ester Hassall, and
Rebecca Martinez—Go-Jii-Yah, 1981.

cost to Petklo. To an outsider, this may not seem like a big deal, but indeed, this was no minor feat. Only a well-liked and well-respected Jicarilla person, like Petklo, could obtain the enthusiastic and eager cooperation of the entire tribe in staging the puberty feasts. In the 1960s she was a tribal court judge and her wisdom and fairness dominated her judgeship. She died about 1978 and will always be remembered.

Other Ollero women who have followed in Petklo's footsteps in providing support for the Ollero Clan are Belle Wells (pages 74, 75) and Rebecca Monarco Martinez (pages 8, 75). Both Belle and Rebecca are lifelong residents of the Jicarilla Reservation. Belle has been considered

Moherita Largo watching the Foot Race from family
brush shelter—Stone Lake, 1976.

Ollero women: (L to R) Petklo Garcia, Helen Lovato, and
June Velarde—Go-Jii-Yah, 1979.

Olleros entering kiva after race—Stone Lake, 1981.

a spiritual leader for her extended family as well as for the entire tribe. She has been a livestock owner, and probably the last stronghold for the raising of sheep. By the late 1970s the majority of Jicarilla sheep raisers had sold their herds and only Belle's herd could be seen along State Highway 536 that runs north and south through the Jicarilla Reservation. Rebecca Monarco Martinez, now 81 years old, is a successful cattle rancher from the southern part of the reservation. Her income has come primarily from the raising of cattle. In a sense, she is another model of the Jicarilla woman who believes in self-reliance, hard work, and has never wavered in her belief in the Jicarilla religion. With the exception of several years when, as a child, she was a tubercular patient at the Jicarilla Mission School during the 1930s, Rebecca has never missed Go-Jii-Yah. Her presence at Go-Jii-Yah has not been limited to

Steve Julian at Stone Lake, 1978.

Paul Callado, Sr. at food stand at Go-Jii-Yah, 1977.

Teepees near the stands at Go-Jii-Yah, 1976.

being a spectator-camper but an active partic-
ipant and supporter of the religious aspects of
the race. Every year she is on the racetrack sur-
rounded by her family and it is no wonder she
was captured in one of the photographs for this
book (page 75). Also pictured in two of the photographs is Helen Lovato (page 8, 77), another
Jicarilla woman who serves as the head of her
extended family. The women portrayed in this
book are only a few of the many Jicarilla
women who are the heads of households.

The Ollero Clan does not have a monopoly
on the "quintessential Jicarilla woman." Jicarilla
Apache society is considered matriarchal, which
means that women are the heads of households
and families. Throughout all the Jicarilla family
groups are women like Petklo, Belle, and Rebecca.
They just don't happen to be pictured in this
book. One woman whose extended family is the
subject of the majority of photographs in this
book is Moherita Veneno Largo (1909–2000),
who also exemplifies the quintessential Jicarilla

Edi Lucero at Go-Jii-Yah, 1980.

woman. Moherita Largo (pages xii, 57, 76) was the matriarch of the Largo/Julian family until her death in December 2000 at the age of 91. Like most of her tribesmen of her time, she came from a family of livestock owners who supplemented their income with farming, the sale of baskets and beadwork, and later on, wages. Moherita has been described by her granddaughter, Geraldine Julian, as a "mentally and physically strong woman, who could do just about anything." Moherita came from the Hole-In-the-Rock and Puerto Springs area of the reservation, where her family has raised sheep and where she ranched and farmed alongside her husband, Pablo Largo. She also found time for making traditional Jicarilla baskets, some of which have received prizes, and *tiswin* (traditional, fermented corn drink) for which she was

Food booth at Go-Jii-Yah, 1979.

Teepee at Go-Jii-Yah, 1978.

Teepee detail at Stone Lake, 1979.

Campfire inside the Julians' brush shelter, 1976.

Ollero flag bearers on horseback on September 14, 1979.

notorious. Most of all she has been remembered by Geraldine as an herbalist and healer. Moherita did not believe in the white man's medicine and drugs. As a healthy woman all her life, she relied on knowledge of Jicarilla herbs and medicinal plants for her pharmacy. She even extended her knowledge of herbal medicine to her livestock. Geraldine remembers one such incident when she saved a valuable red goat, which served as the

"leader" of the sheep and goat herd, that had broken its leg. But most of all Geraldine remembers the numerous times when she was cured as a result of her grandmother's knowledge of medicinal plants. Shona Quintana, Moherita's great granddaughter, describes her as a kind and patient grandmother. To Shona, her grandmother was like the earth and sky; she was always there for her.

BIBLIOGRAPHY

Jicarilla Apache Tribe, Integrated Resource Management Office, "Integrated Resource Management Plan, 1999 Update," unpublished report, 1999, Dulce, New Mexico.

Julian, Geraldine and Larry, interview with author, July 2005, Dulce, New Mexico.

Quintana, Shona, interview with author, July 2005, Dulce, New Mexico.

Tiller, Veronica E. Velarde, *The Jicarilla Apache Tribe: A History*. Revised edition. Albuquerque: BowArrow Publishing Company. 2000.

Tiller, Veronica E. Velarde, editor, *Tiller's Guide to Indian Country: Economic Profiles of American Indian Reservations*. Albuquerque: BowArrow Publishing Company, 2005. pp. 727–33.